MW00626460

EXOTIC BIRDS

EXOTIC BIRDS

Published by Chartwell Books
A Division of Book Sales Inc.
114 Northfield Avenue
Edison, New Jersey 08837
USA

ISBN 0-7858-0969-4

This book is produced by
Quantum Books Ltd
6 Blundell Street
London N7 9BH

Project Manager: Rebecca Kingsley
Project Editor: Judith Millidge
Design/Editorial: David Manson
Andy McColm, Maggie Manson

The material in this publication previously appeared in
Cage and Aviary Birds

QUMSPEB
Set in Futura
Reproduced in Singapore by Eray Scan
Printed in Singapore by Star Standard Industries (Pte) Ltd

Contents

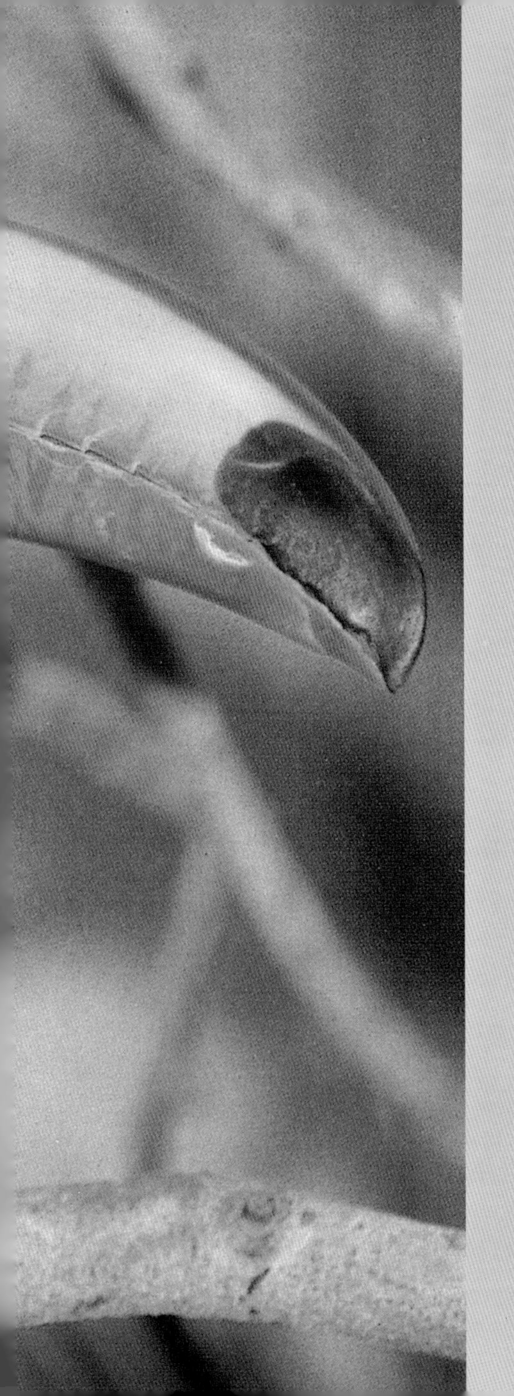

EXQUISITE EXOTIC BIRDS

Even before man had come to live in permanent settlements, he had made companions of bird species. Those first domesticated birds were primarily seen as food sources, but before long, the beautiful songs and wondrous colors of other species earned birds a new position among the creatures that man brought into and near his home.

Timeless Exotic Birds

Birds were among the very first animals that man chose to domesticate. Domestic chickens date back 5,000 years ago to the first settlements in India. But even before that, nomadic tribes used falcons for hunting.

EXOTIC EGYPT

Exotic birds, with their ornamental appeal were originally the province of the great civilizations. Evidence suggests that Egyptian rulers and nobility collected and caged colorful African birds as early as 4000 BC. This was a hobby only for the very rich.

EXOTIC EMPIRES

With the rise of the Greek Empire, exotic birds were cherished as a major symbol of status, power and wealth. Shortly before his death in 323 BC, Alexander the Great brought hundreds of parrots and peafowl back from his last great conquests in India.

Left. The Scarlet Macaw from the savannah regions of Mexico.

Above. Hyacinth Macaws from the rainforests of Brazil.

EXOTIC EUROPE

The Renaissance in Europe (AD1300–1600) brought about a boom in garden aviaries among the wealthy, while the exploration of the New World introduced a previously unknown array of exotic birds to Europe. Columbus brought back a pair of Cuban Amazon parrots for Queen Isabella of Spain from his first voyage, reporting that the native islanders kept several species of domesticated parrots as pets.

EXOTIC INCAS

Long before this first European contact, it was common throughout the Inca Empire for homes to have several tame parrots and parakeets. Certain bird's feathers were part of the tribute that Inca rulers demanded of inland tribes who were under their dominion. Gradually as exploration continued and transportation evolved, exotic birds became available to ever larger numbers of people.

Buying Exotic Birds

The magnificent colors, the wonderfully intelligent eyes, the intriguing ability to fly, the possibility of specialized tricks, such as talking, all combine to give exotic birds a unique appeal.

A FRIEND FOR LIFE

The prospective owner must first be aware of the unique responsibility that comes with bird ownership. The provision of special diet and the danger of disease are all part of that responsibility, which in some species, such as the African Gray Parrot, might extend over the 70 years of the bird's life. Even the canary may be a member of the household for the next 10 years.

FLIGHT SPACE

Space considerations are crucial. Large parrots need very roomy cages and 'playground' areas. Even tiny finches must be allowed enough space for flight. A huge selection of cages are available, ranging from the metal-barred type to glass enclosed showcases. Wood is really only for smaller species as larger birds have destructive chewing habits.

HEALTH CHECK FOR EXOTIC BIRDS

If the bird you plan to purchase shows any of the following symptoms contact a veterinarian before purchasing

- Lackadaisical, withdrawn or sleepy attitude
- Extremely fluffed-up feathers
- Poor balance
- Discharges from the eyes or nostrils
- Protruding breastbone
- Regurgitation or loose droppings
- Bald spots
- Sneezing or coughing

Above. The African Gray Parrot (Psittacus erithacus) is a very long-lived species, with a life expectancy of over 70 years. This must be borne in mind when buying one.

HEALTH CHECK

You should give your retailer an idea of the conditions which the bird will meet in its new home. Reputable retailers will allow a check-up by a veterinarian prior to the sale and a few hours of observation before you buy the bird. The Health Check table opposite lists unhealthy symptoms.

Remember! You are making an investment and commitment that could last many years, so study the bird carefully.

ENDANGERED SPECIES

An increasingly important aspect of any exotic bird is the animal's place of origin. As you will find later in the directory section (see p.16), many species are now considered endangered and threatened in the wild. Buying any bird taken from the wild has serious implications.

Remember! Nearly 80 of the world's 330 parrot species are in danger of extinction in the wild because of illegal trading.

Training Exotic Birds

The first step towards turning your new bird into a family pet must be getting acquainted. Try to see the world through your bird's eyes. It is frightened, alone and in a totally foreign environment.

GENTLE REASSURANCE

To reassure the bird of its safety, move slowly and talk gently. Several days may pass before it begins to calm down. Take full advantage of this time to fully familiarize yourself with the bird's signals, both through its 'speech' and through its body language.

READY TO START

When the bird begins to tolerate your presence close to the cage without being overly agitated, then it is time to begin training it to the hand. No matter how frustrated you may become, you must at all times demonstrate to the bird your overall enjoyment.

Left. The Rose-Breasted Cockatoo is gentle, playful and intelligent with a loud voice.

Above. The Yellow-Fronted Amazon Parrot is easy to train and talks well.

STAY CALM! BE PATIENT!

No session should last more than 15 minutes. This is the maximum attention span for a bird. Never hit a bird as discipline, no matter what it may do. Birds simply do not have the capacity to accept force as anything other than a threat. Patience and gentleness are the only things to which they will respond.

Remember! For your own safety wear leather gloves to work with medium-sized birds, such as the smaller parrots and hold a stick for cockatoos and macaws.

TRAINING TO HAND

Begin with your hand inside the cage, where the bird feels secure. Moving very slowly and talking gently, push your hand or stick against the bird where its chest and legs meet. The bird should jump onto your hand. Offer the bird a treat when it perches on your hand. Eventually, when you have mastered this technique, slowly pull your hand out of the cage with the bird on it. At first, the bird may jump off, but be patient and continue the process until the bird is relaxed on your hand outside the cage.

Exercising Exotic Birds

Daily exercise periods are necessary to maintain the bird's health, and these should allow for all the activities that the bird would engage in if it were still living in the wild.

PHYSICAL EXERCISE

In addition to adequate flight space within its enclosure, the bird should be allowed some free flight outside the cage. A room in the house, most likely the one in which the bird is regularly housed in its cage, will serve this function well. All poisonous plants should be removed; mirrors, windows and anything the bird may fly 'through' or attack should be covered. Close all doors and windows to prevent unexpected escape routes. Provide the bird with a secure and serene atmosphere, and leave the cage door open for voluntary returns. The bird's legs and feet are kept in tone by perching and climbing activities. Bird's beaks grow continuously throughout their lives. Provide cuttlefish, lava stones, nuts and seeds to help wear it down.

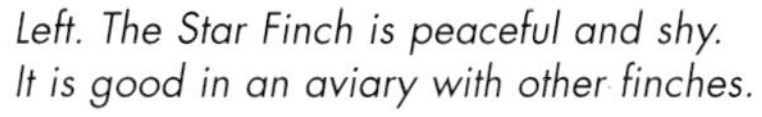

Left. The Star Finch is peaceful and shy. It is good in an aviary with other finches.

Above. The Zebra Finch from Australia is sociable and easily tamed.

MENTAL EXERCISE

Keep the bird stimulated and physically sharp with games and toys, sights and sounds. Smaller birds enjoy mirrors, ladders and swings. Above all, birds thrive on companionship. For the solitary pet, this means time every day with its owner. Companionship aids such as tape recordings will help give the bird a mental work out, but nothing replaces time together. Birds have many ways of telling us if they are not getting enough mental stimulation. All the activities listed in the following table are warning signals.

SYMPTOMS OF A BORED BIRD

Any of the following symptoms indicate your bird needs more mental exercise:

- Feather picking and plucking
- Non-stop, repetitive motions
- Aggression beyond normal
- Loss of interest in play
- Cessation of talking/singing
- Toe chewing

EXOTIC BIRD SPECIES

Key to symbols

The following icons are used throughout the directory to help provide a snapshot of the care that each species requires.

Diet

Insect-eaters

Fruit-eaters

Seed-eaters

Sociability

Solitary

Pairs

Groups

Voice

Singing

Talking

Endangered status

Monitored

Concern

Protected

THROUGHOUT THE DIRECTORY

The common name for the species is given first, followed by the scientific name.

RINGNECK PARAKEET PSITTACULA KRAMERI MANILLENSIS

These birds need a generous aviary with a temperate, protected area. They are green in color, with a black collar and red shine behind the collar. An ideal aviary pet which may talk and can live for half a century.

Alternative names Indian Ringneck, Rose-Fringed Parakeet.
Size 16in.
Distribution Africa, Asia, China.
Habitat Gardens, parks, farmland, woodland and timbered areas.
Diet Ripening fruit, grain, parrot mixture, greenery, non-fatty seeds.

PLUM-HEADED PARAKEET PSITTACULA CYANOCEPHALA

These birds need an aviary to themselves if breeding is to be successful, which should have a frost-free protected area. The males have plum-colored heads and black neck ring. They get on well with other small birds and have a tolerable voice.

Alternative name None.
Size 15in.
Distribution India, Nepal, Bhutan, Sri Lanka, West Bengal.
Habitat Jungles, cultivated areas, forests.
Diet Grain, fruit, greenery.

ALEXANDRINE PARAKEET PSITTACULA EUPATRIA

These birds have a prominent black collar around the neck with a mostly green body color. They require a large, metal aviary. They can be quite tame and fair talkers when confined to a cage. Successful breeding will occur only if ample space is provided.

Alternative name None.
Size 20in.
Distribution Southeast Asia.
Habitat Forests, parks, cultivated land.
Diet Seeds and fruit.

CANARY-WINGED PARAKEET BROTOGERIS VERSICOLORUS CHIRIRI

Primarily green with bright yellow, these birds should only be kept as pairs until brooding time. They need protecting from frost and to have bathing and climbing facilities. Friendly, very tame birds and good breeders, they can be jealous of other pets.

Alternative name None.
Size 10in.
Distribution Amazon, Brazil, Bolivia, Paraguay, Peru and Argentina.
Habitat Forests and towns.
Diet Parrot mix, cereal seeds, fruit especially bananas and greenery.

BARRED PARAKEET BOLBORHYNCHUS LINEOLA

Green with black shell markings on its body, these birds are sensitive to frost. They need shaded areas and strong branches to slide along. They are tame, gentle and tolerant, with a pleasant voice.

Alternative name Lineolated Parakeet, Catherine Parakeet.
Size 6½ in.
Distribution Mexico, Panama, Peru and Colombia.
Habitat Deep mountain forests in hollow trees, usually in groups.
Diet Oats, millet spray, sunflower seed kernels, fresh twigs, fruit and insects.

BOURKE'S PARAKEET NEOPHEMA BOUKII

These birds have pink and gray mottling on their face and underside of the body, with a blue area above the beak. They need a warm, dry environment to live in. They nest in tree hollows or nesting boxes.

Alternative name None.
Size 8½ in.
Distribution Central America.
Habitat Prairie-type areas that feature acacia bushes. The species is somewhat nocturnal and live in small flocks, nesting in hollow trees.
Diet Seeds, fruit, insects.

CRIMSON-WINGED PARAKEET APROSMICTUS ERYTHROPTERUS ERYTHROPTERUS

The male is bright green, darker on the back with bright red wing coverts. The female has only a small patch of red. Adults are not good community birds. They nest in tree hollows, particularly eucalyptus.

Alternative name None.
Size 13in.
Distribution Northeast Australia and New Guinea.
Habitat Open forest areas.
Diet Seeds and nuts.

MONK PARAKEET MYIOPSITTA MONACHUS

These birds have green bodies with grayish-blue head and breast. For successful breeding, they need to have a generous amount of space with lots of shrubbery. They are peaceful but have an exaggerated reputation as a screamer.

Alternative names Quaker or Gray-Breasted Parakeet.
Size 12in.
Distribution Brazil, Argentina, New York, New Jersey, Florida, Virginia.
Habitat Lowland, woods, farmland, savannahs, woods, orchards.
Diet Mixed grain, fruit, carrots, greenery.

EASTERN ROSELLA PLATYCEREUS EXIMIUS

A bird with a bright red head, shoulders, and breast; not as brilliant in the female. White cheek marks in the male, dirty white in the female. The tail is green in the center, then blue, edged in white. There are red feathers under the tail. These birds should be kept in pairs in an aviary with bathing facilities. They have a loud voice and are aggressive towards other birds but make excellent breeders and foster parents. They can damage cornfields and orchards as they are partial to ground, living in large groups or pairs.

Alternative names Red Rosella, Golden-Mantled Rosella.
Size $12^{1}/_{2}$ in.
Distribution Southeastern Australia, Tasmania, New Zealand.
Habitat Open grassy terrain.
Diet Grass and weed seeds, grain, apples, carrots, greenery.

LESSER SULPHUR-CRESTED COCKATOO CACATUA SULPHUREA

These birds are mainly white overall with black legs and beak, and a crest of yellow or orange. Provide a metal aviary with a frost-free, sheltered area for these birds who like to bathe in rain or under a shower.

Alternative name None.
Size 14in.
Distribution Indonesia, Sulawesi, Lombok, Sumba, Sumbawa, Flores.
Habitat Forests and farmland.
Diet Parrot mixture, sunflower seeds, corn, wheat millet, pine nuts, berries.

LEADBEATER'S COCKATOO CACTUA LEADBEATERI

They have a prominent large broad crest with red, white and yellow stripes and the body is mostly white with a pinkish tint. These birds need a large aviary. Birds bred in captivity are very tame and fair talkers.

Alternative name Major Mitchell's Cockatoo.
Size 15 1/4 in.
Distribution Australia.
Habitat Thick brush of eucalyptus subspecies, in pairs and flocks, usually as families.
Diet Seeds and fruit.

UMBRELLA COCKATOO CACATUA ALBA

White body, with black eyes, beak and legs. These birds need a large aviary. They are friendly, quiet, beautiful, gentle and easy to tame. Can be long-lived and are not good takers. Breeding in an aviary is possible, but rare.

Alternative names Great White Cockatoo, White-crested Cockatoo.
Size 18in.
Distribution Moluccas.
Habitat Forests, near farms in pairs or small groups.
Diet Seeds, fruit.

MOLUCCAN COCKATOO CACTUA MOLUCCENSIS

They have a ruffled appearance due to the large feathers. Body colors vary from white to salmon or deep pink. Successful breeding requires a large aviary. They are good imitators, gentle and affectionate.

Alternative name Salmon-Crested Cockatoo, Rose-Crested Cockatoo.
Size 20in.
Distribution Moluccas, Ceram, Sapurua, Haruko, Amboina.
Habitat Coastal areas and forests in small flocks
Diet Fruit, coconuts, insects, sunflower seeds, wheat, corn, oats, peanuts.

GREAT PALM COCKATOO PROBOSCIGER ATERRIMUS

The largest of all cockatoos, they are grayish-black with a bare red facial patch. Aviaries need to be able to withstand the strong beak. These birds are usually gentle but have dramatic displays when choosing territories for breeding.

Alternative name None.
Size 24in.
Distribution Australia, New Guinea and surrounding islands.
Habitat Tropical and monsoon rain forests bordering on savannah, in flocks.
Diet Seeds, nuts.

ROSE-BREASTED COCKATOO CACATUA ROSEICAPPILUS

The most common cockatoo with deep pink body, light pink crest and gray elsewhere. For successful breeding, dampen nest boxes regularly. These are gentle, playful, intelligent birds who are good talkers with a loud voice.

Alternative names Galah Cockatoo, Roseate Cockatoo.
Size 15in.
Distribution Australia and Tasmania.
Habitat Savannah, open country, farmland, eucalyptus woodland, gardens.
Diet Parrot mix, cereal seeds, fruit, greenery, insects, oats, wheat, millet.

COCKATIEL NYMPHICUS HOLLANDICUS

They resemble cockatoos, but have a long tail. The most common coloring has a yellow throat and head with a grayish-blue crest and beak. Allow tame birds in a room cage to have daily free flights. Readily breed in roomy aviaries. Graceful and peaceable bird which can talk and mimic, living to 25 years.

Alternative name None.
Size 14in.
Distribution Australia and Tasmania.
Habitat Savannahs, grassland, near water, usually in pairs.
Diet Grain mixes for parrots, canary seed, millet, hemp, apples, carrots.

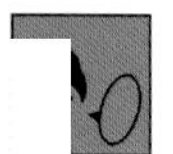

PEACH-FACED LOVEBIRD AGAPORNIS ROSEICOLLIS

Mostly bright, accented by a pinkish forehead, cheeks, chin, throat and below; blue on rump and uppertail-coverts. Yellow beak. Dry room air creates hatching problems. Small, easy to tame, noisy, aggressive towards other species. Garden aviaries need covered areas with sleeping boxes.

Alternative name None.
Size 7in.
Distribution Southwest Africa.
Habitat Near water in savannahs.
Diet Cereal seeds, sunflower/safflower seeds, greenstuff, fruit, millet spray.

FISCHER'S LOVEBIRD AGAPORNIS PERSONATA FISCHERI

Body is shades of green, with orange forehead and cheeks and a red beak. Best kept in pairs, these birds are sensitive to frost and require bathing dishes in their cage. They are attractive birds, easy to accommodate and sociable.

Alternative name None.
Size 6in.
Distribution Africa.
Habitat Savannahs.
Diet Cereal seeds, grain mixes, fruit, sunflower and safflower seeds and greenery.

MASKED LOVEBIRD AGAPORNIS PERSONATA PERSONATA

Dark brown head, yellow collar and breast with a red bill. Keep as a pair in an aviary with a sleeping box and shallow bathing dish. These birds are susceptible to frost and need to gnaw fresh branches for building. Quiet birds with distinctive coloration.

Alternative name White Eye-Ring Lovebird, Yellow-Collared Lovebird.
Size 6in.
Distribution Tanzania, Kenya.
Habitat Nomadic. Grassy prairies with some trees.
Diet Cereal seeds, grain mixes, fruit, greenery sunflower and safflower seeds.

PEACH-FRONTED CONURE ARATINGA AUREA

Yellowish-orange head bordered with blue and a dark green rump and neck. They require bathing facilities and roosting boxes. Easy to breed and have a loud voice. Tolerates other species only outside the brooding period.

Alternative name Golden-Crowned Conure.
Size 11in.
Distribution Brazil, Bolivia, Paraguay, Argentina.
Habitat Savannah woods, and open country.
Diet Grass seeds, hemp, oats, live worms, berries, apples, grain mix.

SUN CONURE ARATINGA SOLSTIALIS

Mainly yellow with orange head and belly, large primaries edged in blue, small primaries green. Charcoal beak. Newly imported birds must be kept at temperatures of above 68°F. Susceptible to feather plucking and gives shrill, two-note screeches.

Alternative name None.
Size 12in.
Distribution South America.
Habitat Forests, savannahs, palm groves.
Diet Parrot mix, cereal seeds, fruit, nuts, greenery, blossoms.

CACTUS CONURE ARATINGA ACTORUM

Brownish-green on head, turning olive down back and on wings. Orange rust below breast. They have a friendly, even affectionate, personality and stay relatively peaceful with other conures.

Alternative name None.
Size 11in.
Distribution Brazil.
Habitat South American rainforest.
Diet Cactus seeds in the wild, fruit and berries.

BLUE-CROWNED CONURE ARATINGA ACUTICAUDATA

Green body with yellow showing underneath. Forehead and part of head showing blue. It is essential to have fruit and berries in their diet. These are intelligent and affectionate birds with a strong voice. They may learn to talk.

Alternative name None.
Size 14 1/2 in.
Distribution Venezuela, Brazil, Colombia.
Habitat Forest near farmland, fruit trees, sometimes in large flocks.
Diet Seeds, fruit, berries.

WHITE-EARED CONURE PYRRHURA LEUCOTIS

The neck and throat of this bird are bright blue, with whitish ear coverts. The head and tail are brown, wings are bluer and green. Immatures need supplements of soaked stale white bread, cooked corn, boiled potatoes, oats, carrot strips, fresh twigs and leaf buds. A popular conure which is easy to tame.

Alternative name None.
Size 9in.
Distribution Venezuela, Brazil.
Habitat High tropical and subtropical trees in small groups.
Diet Insects, larvae, termites, fruit, seeds.

RED BELLIED CONURE PYRRHURA FRONTALIS

The body is green with gray-green chin and breast. Wing coverts are bluish, the tail is copper at base and end. For good breeding results, keep a pair on their own in a quiet, protected aviary. They are easy to tame, lively and inquisitive.

Alternative name Maroon-Bellied Conure.
Size 10in.
Distribution South America, Paraguay, Brazil and Argentina.
Habitat Forests, farmland, orchards, corn fields.
Diet Parrot mix, pine nuts, cereal seeds, greenery, millet, fruit, insects and larvae.

NANDAYA CONURE NANDAYAS NENDAY

These birds are green with a blackish cap, upper throat and below the eyes. The wings are bluish-black and the thighs red. These birds are much too loud to keep indoors. They can be kept together with finches and they like to bathe or hop in a rain shower.

Alternative name Black-Headed Conure, Black-Masked Conure.
Size 12in.
Distribution Argentina, Paraguay, Bolivia, Mato Grosso.
Habitat Savannahs, woods, palm country, rice fields.
Diet Grain, seeds, fruit.

BLUE-WINGED CONUR PYRRHURA PICTA

There is a prominent black collar around the neck with an additional pink layer at the back. The body is mostly green with a reddish shoulder patch. They require a large, metal aviary. When raised under cage conditions, they can be quite tame. They are fair talkers if confined to a cage.

Alternative name Painted Conure.
Size 20in.
Distribution Southeast Asia.
Habitat Forests, parks and cultivated land.
Diet Seeds, fruit.

CELESTIAL PARROTLET FORPUS COELESTI

Green, plus blue on the wings, on rump and on a narrow band along the back of the neck. Newly imported birds must be kept at room temperature. Pairs must be alone to breed. An ideal cage bird which can be kept with several pairs if no breeding is expected.

Alternative name Pacific Parrotlet.
Size $4^3/4$ in.
Distribution Tropical areas of South America.
Habitat Woody areas in colonies.
Diet Fruit.

GREEN-RUMPED PARROTLET FORPUS PASSERINUS

All green, brighter on the face, forehead and rump, lighter underneath. Turquoise tint on wing, pale beak. Need a varied diet of seeds, fruit and vegetables

Alternative name None.
Size $4^3/4$ in.
Distribution Venezuela, Trinidad, Colombia.
Habitat Wooded areas.
Diet Sunflower and safflowers seeds, cereals, nuts, greenery, dates and figs.

RED LORY EOS BORNEA

Red with blue vent and undertail coverts. Black and red wings, blue coverts. Red eyes, beak orange and legs charcoal. Sudden changes in diet can lead to bacterial changes within the gut, which could precipitate a fatal bout of enterotoxaemia.

Alternative name Mollucan.
Size $12\frac{1}{4}$ in.
Distribution Indonesia.
Habitat Coastal and mountain forests.
Diet Nectar, pollen, fruit, supplemented with seeds and grain.

CHATTERING LORY LORIUS GARRULUS

Glowing, deep red overall with wings and thighs brown-green. Keep in pairs and provide bathing facilities. They have loud voices, imitate well and are messy eaters. Can be aggressive towards other pairs of same species.

Alternative name None.
Size 12in.
Distribution Moluccan Islands.
Habitat Forest regions, around flowering coconuts and palm trees.
Diet Nectar, fruit, greenery, seeds. Supplement with Vitamin A to avoid candidiasis and provide pollen.

AFRICAN GRAY PARROT PSITTACUS ERITHACUS

Body is dove-gray with lighter gray feathered face, red tail and under coverts and a black beak. Always check newly imported birds for bacterial infections, especially salmonella. Probably the best talking parrot and an affectionate bird.

Alternative name Gray Parrot.
Size 14in.
Distribution Central Africa.
Habitat Forests, savannahs, mangroves.
Diet Parrot food, nuts, grains, fruit and greenery.

BLUE-FRONTED AMAZON PARROT AMAZONA AESTIVA

They have a green body with bluish forehead and yellow throat, cheeks and crown. It is essential that they are given fruit and berries, and wood for chewing. They are excellent talkers, mimic well, and are responsive to training.

Alternative name None.
Size 16in.
Distribution Brazil, Bolivia, Paraguay, Argentina.
Habitat Tropical woods, bush country. Nomadic.
Diet Fruit, nuts, berries, corncobs, parrot mix, sunflower seeds, half-ripe wheat.

ELECTUS PARROT ELECTUS RORATUS

The sexes are differently colored. Males are mostly green, females are red. The male's upper mandible is coral while the female's is black. Imported birds need warm indoor aviaries, fresh water and have a high vitamin A requirement. Likely to refuse all food at first but will settle down with partner.

Alternative name Grand Electus.
Size 15in.
Distribution Moluccas, Ceram, Solomon Islands, New Guinea, Australia.
Habitat Forest and mountain regions.
Diet Sunflower seeds, millet spray, cooked rice, vegetables, peanuts.

YELLOW-FRONTED AMAZON PARROT AMAZONA OCHROCEPHALA

Green with golden crown and red wing coverts. These birds need a large, strong cage and to be kept in pairs in an outdoor aviary. They are easy to train and talk well, but do not mimic. Likes human company.

Alternative name Yellow-Crowned Amazon.
Size $15^3/4$in.
Distribution Mexico, Central America, California, Florida.
Habitat Forests, woods, savannahs, fields, in pairs or flocks.
Diet Sunflower seeds, corn, wheat, oats, peanuts, parrot mix, fruit, berries.

MEXICAN RED-HEADED PARROT AMAZONA VIRIDIGENALIS

A green bird with black edges on feathers. A red cap covers down to the eyes and there is a blue crown. It is essential to supply fruit and berries, as well, as wood for chewing. Gentle and popular birds, they are good talkers.

Alternative name Green-Cheeked Amazon Parrot.
Size 13in.
Distribution Northern Mexico.
Habitat Forests, lowlands, near water. Forages in cypress and acacia trees.
Diet Sunflower seeds, fruit berries, millet, hazelnuts, hemp, oats, boiled corn.

BLUE AND YELLOW MACAW ARA ARARAUNA

Turquoise wings and back with golden belly, neck and breast. These birds have strong beaks which can find weaknesses in the design and construction of their cages. They are affectionate, loyal, gentle, and intelligent, capable of learning tricks and talking.

Alternative name Blue-and-Gold Macaw.
Size 36in.
Distribution Panama, Paraguay.
Habitat Close to water forests, savannahs, open country and swamps.
Diet Leaves, seeds, fruit, nuts, cheese, parrot food, greenery.

SCARLET MACAW ARA MACAO

The body is deep red, shoulders and wings yellow. Primaries and tail coverts blue. Provide fresh branches for occupation. A sociable bird, usually monogamous in pairs, and affectionate. They can be noisy when bored.

Alternative name None.
Size 33 1/2 in.
Distribution Mexico, Central America, northern South America.
Habitat Light woodland, savannah, humid areas, in pairs.
Diet Oranges, bananas, nuts, berries, carrots, calcium, tomatoes, fresh twigs.

MILITARY MACAW ARA MILITARIS

An olive colored bird with a red forehead, blue upper coverts and a rump of bluish-red primary feathers. Charcoal beak. Barrels or drums for pairs. An easily tamed, friendly bird with a moderate talking ability.

Alternative name Great Green Macaw.
Size 25 1/2in.
Distribution Mexico to Argentina.
Habitat Dry forest and open woodland, in pairs or small flocks.
Diet Nuts, berries, fruit, greens.

HYACINTH MACAW ANODORHYNCHUS HYACINTHINUS

The largest living parrot, now rare and expensive. The body is a deep blue-purple accented by yellow eye ring and bold yellow along the mandible bottom. They need a very strong cage and their perches changed regularly. Tame with trusted people and close pair bonding.

Alternative name None.
Size 39 1/2in.
Distribution Brazil, Bolivia, Paraguay.
Habitat Highlands, in palm forests, near rivers and lakes, in swamps.
Diet Palm nuts, fruit and snails, fruit, sunflowers seeds, corn ears.

GREEN-WINGED MACAW ARA CHLOROPTERA

This bird has a dark red head with green shoulder coverts and large upper-wing. Blue wings, rump and tail tip. Provide branches, as their bills can be devasting to woodwork. Quiet, tame, intelligent, and kind to children and pets, but easily frightened.

Alternative name Marron Macaw.
Size 36in.
Distribution Panama, Paraguay, Argentina, Bolivia.
Habitat Hilly country and virgin forest, in pairs and small groups.
Diet Parrot food with fruit, greenery, fresh corn, sunflower seed kernels.

RAINBOW LORIKEET TRICHOGLOSSUS HAEMATODUS MOLUCCANUS

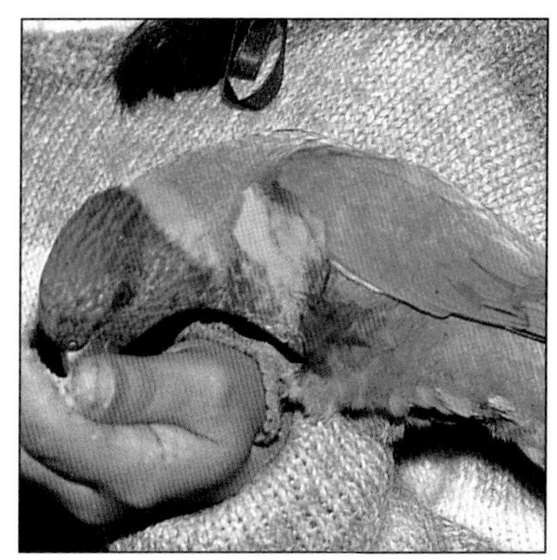

Patched in a variety of colors. Violet to blue head and belly, yellow on back of head and mixed green shades on back and wings. Breast red with yellow. They do not get on with other species. Should be kept in pairs in a long aviary with a roomy night shelter. Prolific breeders.

Alternative name Swainson's Lorikeet, Blue Mountain Lorikeet.
Size 12in.
Distribution Australia, Pacific.
Habitat Lowlands, savannahs, woodlands, near water.
Diet Fruit, insects, pollen nectar, oats, spray millet, apples, grapes, mealworms.

BUDGERIGAR MELOPSITTACUS UNDULATUS

Green with a yellow forehead and cheeks. Horizontal black and yellow bands on back. Many mutations. Indoor birds need iodine. They are inexpensive, easy to care for, sociable and quick to tame, and can prove talented talkers. Brought to Europe in 19th century, now one of the most popular cage birds.

Alternative name None.
Size 7in.
Distribution Australia, Tasmania. Nomadic.
Habitat Grassland, close to water.
Diet Millet, canary grass seeds, oats, greenery, carrots, sweet apples.

DOMESTIC CANARY SERINUS CANARIUS DOMESTICUS

These birds have several forms which have been developed for body type, coloration or singing ability. There are three color forms: yellow, white and buff, each having a different feather texture. If a singing bird is required, then choose a cock no matter what the breed. Can be home bred in a breeding cage with a nesting pan inside.

Alternative name None.
Size 8in.
Distribution Does not occur in the wild.
Habitat Cages and aviaries.
Diet Canary seed mixture, with niger seeds, red rape and greenery.

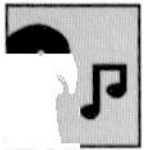

WHITE-HEADED MUNIA LONCHURA MAJA

They have a chestnut-colored body with white head, black underparts. It has fast-growing nails which should be trimmed twice a year. They need fresh bathwater daily and they are much in demand around the world.

Alternative names Mannikan, Nun.
Size 5in.
Distribution Malay Peninsula.
Habitat Grassland, sometimes in large flocks.
Diet Insects, cuttlebone, weed seeds, egg food, greens, stale bread soaked in water or milk.

GREEN SINGING FINCH SERINUS MOZAMBICUS

Greenish-gray upperparts, yellow rump underneath, yellow eyebrow, throat and chin. Breeding will be successful if a large cage or indoor aviary is provided, and where a warm temperature can be maintained. Long-lived, hardy and bright. The male can be aggressive towards small finches and waxbills.

Alternative name Yellow-Eyed Canary.
Size 5in.
Distribution Africa, south of the Sahara.
Habitat Gardens, parks, woodland.
Diet Canary and live food.

ZEBRA FINCH TAENIOPYGIA (POEPHILA) GUTTATA

Grayish-blue on head and neck, turning to grayish-brown on back and wings. Red beak, sides orangish-red with white round marks, black band under eye marks. Separate cocks and hens during the winter and do not breed females until they are 9–10 months old. Hardy, sociable, and easily tamed, they are prolific breeders in outdoor aviaries.

Alternative name None.
Size 4in.
Distribution Australia.
Habitat Open woods and grassy areas, arid interiors near water.
Diet Millets, canary seed, greenery.

CUT-THROAT FINCH AMADINA FASCIATA

Light tanned in color with a black bar on each feather, gray-brown on tail and primaries. They need a steady supply of minerals and cuttlefish bone as female is susceptible to egg binding. Only keep with species of same size as they will destroy nests of smaller birds. Good breeders.

Alternative name Ribbon Finch.
Size 5in.
Distribution Africa, south of Sahara.
Habitat Savannah, bush, farmland.
Diet Insects, sprouted seeds.

RED-HEADED FINCH AMADINA ERYTHROCEPHALA

Resembles Cut-Throat Finch – body light fawn, feathers marked with black bars, chocolate underside, gray tail, whitish throat with red band on front of neck. Seldom builds own nests. House as a single pair in a roomy aviary and provide a peaceful place to breed.

Alternative name Red-Browed Finch, Paradise Sparrow.
Size $5^{1}/4$in.
Distribution South Africa to Angola.
Habitat Open country with bushes, in colonies.
Diet Seeds, insects.

SPICE FINCH LONCHURA PUNCTULATA

Spicy brown color, darker brown on head, lighter brown and white on underparts. Hens have a tendency to suffer from egg binding. Appealing nature, they are easy to please, and can be housed in either an aviary or glass enclosure. Almost always in motion.

Alternative name Spice Bird.
Size $4^{1}/_{2}$in.
Distribution India, Sri Lanka, Taiwan, Hainan, Sulawesi, Philippines, Australia, south China.
Habitat Grassland, parks and gardens.
Diet Seeds, insects.

MELBA FINCH PYTILIA MELBA

Scarlet-orange forehead, chin and throat. Rest of head gray, underside has white streaks and spots. Scarlet beak. Prevent pairs from throwing young out of the nest by feeding rich variety of insects and small seeds. Keep only one pair in a community aviary.

Alternative name Crimson-Faced Waxbill.
Size 5in.
Distribution Africa, south of Sahara.
Habitat Thorny thickets.
Diet Seeds, vitamins, minerals, insects.

BICHENO'S FINCH STIZOPTERA (POEPHILA) BICHENOVII

Smallest of the Australian grass finches. Face, throat and underparts white with black bands across breast and neck. House indoors in autumn and winter. Leave a leaf-mould compost heap in a corner to let them look for insects. These are friendly, peaceful birds.

Alternative name Double-Barred Finch, Owl Finch.
Size 3in.
Distribution Australia.
Habitat Long grass and scrub, near water, parks and gardens.
Diet Insects, seed mixture. Drinks by sucking.

STRAWBERRY FINCH AMANDAVA AMANDAVA

Reddish-brown with scarlet on sides of head, throat, underparts and rump, and black on tail. These birds can be trouble-some to other birds in the breeding season; house separately at this time. Live food essential all year. Very suitable for breeding, males sings all year round.

Alternative name Red Avadavat, Tiger Finch.
Size 4in.
Distribution India, Pakistan, Nepal, Moluccas, Indonesia, China.
Habitat Scrub, jungle, cultivated areas
Diet Seeds, insects, live food.

STAR FINCH NEOCHIMA (BATHILDA) RUFICAUDA

Scarlet face with small white spots extending to and becoming larger on the light olive breast. House indoors at room temperature during the winter. Peaceful, shy and quiet, good in aviary with other small finches. Spends a lot of time on the ground.

Alternative name None.
Size 4 1/2in.
Distribution Northern Australia.
Habitat Tall grass, rice and cane fields, bushes, near water.
Diet Insects, seeds, greens, vitamins, minerals and rearing foods.

GOULDIAN FINCH CHLOEBIA GOULDIAE

Scarlet head, bordered with narrow black band, followed by a broad turquoise band. Throat and chin black. Breast purple, followed by golden-yellow. Neck, wings and tail green. Need a dry, warm aviary with humidity at 70%. Sociable birds.

Alternative name None.
Size 5 1/2in.
Distribution Northern Australia.
Habitat Grassy plains with trees, mangrove swamps and thickets, near water.
Diet Protein-rich foods, vitamins, minerals sprouted seeds.

BENGALESE FINCH LONCHURA STRIATA DOMESTICA

Bred in a wide range of colors, some having a crest. Dark brown are called Self Chocolate, lighter brown Self Fawns, pied variants Fawn and White, Chestnut variant in pied and self forms, and pure white called Self White. Leave in peace while breeding. Suitable as aviary and cage bird. Compatible, breeds readily.

Alternative names Society Finch.
Size 5in.
Distribution Not found in the wild; bred from Sharp-Tailed Munia.
Habitat Oldest-known domesticated caged bird.
Diet Millet, cereal seeds, greenery.

RED-EARED WAXBILL ESTRILDA TROLODYTES

Mouse-brown with some gray on head, crimson eye line and beak. Black tail and underside, and throat whitish with a pink sheen. Needs a lot of insects and fresh bathing water daily. A busy bird with a shrill song.

Alternative names Gray Waxbill, Coralbeak.
Size 4in.
Distribution Africa.
Habitat Semi-arid areas and swamps.
Diet Millet, seeds and live food.

GOLDEN-BREASTED WAXBILL AMANDAVA SUBFLORA

Olive-brown upperparts, yellow below, red rump, orange breast, red streak through eyes with a coral red beak. Can be aggressive towards other birds during breeding season, so provide enough plant life for hiding places in aviary. Keep in an outside aviary in summer, in warmer area in winter. Breeding in captivity is rare.

Alternative names Zebra Waxbill.
Size $3^{1}/_{2}$in.
Distribution Africa, south of Sahara.
Habitat Grassland, cultivated areas.
Diet Seeds, insects.

BLACK-CAPPED WAXBILL AEGINTHA TEMPORALIS

Mostly gray, with a prominent black cap, as well as black primaries and tail feathers, red on rump and uppertail coverts. Needs an outdoor, planted aviary where the birds can catch live food, which enhances their lives and promotes breeding. Must be kept warm at all times. Can be quite tame, although has restless personality.

Alternative names None.
Size 4in.
Distribution South Africa.
Habitat Forested areas. Usually in groups.
Diet Seeds, small insects.

ORANGE-CHEEKED WAXBILL ESTRILDA MELPODA

Body grayish-brown, with lighter, gray or brown and orange cheeks. Underside almost white, rump orangish, tail black and red beak. Needs aphids, ant eggs and mealworms during rearing period. Prolific breeders, suitable for cage and aviary. Only the male sings. Can be nervous but have pleasing personalities.

Alternative names None.
Size 4in.
Distribution Africa, Caribbean.
Habitat Grassland.
Diet Millet, seeds.

ST HELENA WAXBILL ESTRILDA ASTRILD

Brown body with dark bars on upper parts, pinkish on underparts. Crimson eye band and red beak. Undertail coverts black. Needs live food during breeding season. While breeding, house just one pair of birds in an aviary to avoid troubles.

Alternative names Common Waxbill.
Size 4 1/2in.
Distribution Africa, south of Sahara, Madagascar, Mauritius, St Helena, Portugal, Spain.
Habitat Grassland, cultivated areas.
Diet Millet, seeds.

VIOLET-EARED WAXBILL GRANATINA GRANATINA

Bright chestnut with violet ear patches, blue forehead and tail coverts, purple beak with red tip. Needs live food throughout breeding season and a roomy aviary. Will not survive in temperatures below 70°F.

Alternative names None.
Size 4 1/2in.
Distribution Africa.
Habitat Thorn scrub country and arid areas.
Diet Small seeds, live food.

AFRICAN SILVERBILL LONCHURA CANTANS

Sandy/taupe brown with subdued whitish stripes. These birds should not be disturbed during breeding, not even for nest control. Place in unheated area indoors during winter. The male has a musical song.

Alternative names Warbling Silverbill.
Size 4 1/2in.
Distribution Africa.
Habitat Savannahs, farmland near villages, under roofs, in walls of huts.
Diet Greens, millet, spray millet.

S P A R R O W S

JAVA SPARROW PADDA ORYZIVORA

Steel-blue body with black head and tail, white cheeks, pink eye ring and beak, which is very large. Keeping Java sparrows is illegal in some parts of the USA, as escaped birds could seriously threaten agriculture. Ideal aviary inhabitants.

Alternative names Rice Bird, Paddy Bird, Temple Bird.
Size $5^1/2$in.
Distribution Java, Bali, Sri Lanka, Burma, Zanzibar, St Helena.
Habitat Rice and bamboo fields.
Diet Canary and millet seeds, millet sprays, greenery, soft food.

DIAMOND SPARROW STAGONOPLURA GUTTATA

Grayish-brown underparts and wings, with gray face, black lores and black band across chest. Flanks black with white round spots, tail black and upper-tail coverts red. Red beak. Tend to get fat if kept confined; keep only one pair per aviary. Can bully smaller birds and interfere with their nest, killing the young.

Alternative names None.
Size 5in.
Distribution Eastern Australia.
Habitat Woods, grassland, always near water.
Diet Insects, seeds.

RED-CHEEKED CORDON BLEU URAEGINTHUS BENGALUS

Mousey upper parts and abdomen blended with blue on face, throat, breast, uppertail coverts and sides. Crimson ear patches and beak with black tip. Tail a duller blue. Towards the end of the summer, house in an indoor aviary or large cage. Imported birds must be carefully acclimatized. Lively aviary bird.

Alternative names None.
Size 5in.
Distribution Africa.
Habitat Open country, cultivated areas.
Diet Ant eggs, aphids, spiders.

CHINESE PAINTED QUAIL EXCALFACTORIA CHINENSIS

White cheeks with black border, throat black. Broad white band across upper breast and neck. Lower chest deep chocolate brown. Yellow legs and black beak. Hens lack the black and white markings.

Alternative names Painted Quail, Blue-Breasted Quail.
Size 4 1/2in.
Distribution India, southern China.
Habitat Swamps and grassland.
Diet Heavy rations of live insects. Soaked bread, commercial rearing food, ant pupae, poppy seed and greenery should all be offered when rearing.

COMMON PEAFOWL PAVO CRISTATUS

Male is known for its train of upper tail feathers, spread out as a fan by raising tail underneath. Neck and breast bright blue, lower back bronze-green with scallops and upper tail coverts bronze-green with purplish and black center.

Alternative names Indian Peafowl, Peacock.
Size 90in.
Distribution Sri Lanka, India, Pakistan.
Habitat Deciduous forests, semi-open country by hillside streams. Farmland foragers.
Diet Seeds, grain, lentils, ground nuts, greenery.

HELMETED GUINEAFOWL NUMIDA MITRATA

Distinguished by the bony casque (the helmet) on top of its head, covered with a sheath of keratin and well-developed blue and/or red wattles. Needs shelter and outside habitat. Lays eggs in scrape on the ground.

Alternative names None.
Size 23in.
Distribution Chad to Ethiopia, Zaire, Kenya, Uganda.
Habitat Open grassland. May forage in flocks of several hundred.
Diet Bulbs, tubers, berries, insects and snails.

GREAT ARGUS PHEASANT ARGUSIANUS ARGUS

Their distinguishing feature is their tremendous tail. Plumage showing complicated pattern of chestnut, brown, white, black and gray spots, ocelli and bars. Needs shelter as cannot tolerate frost. Male fans his wing feathers at climax of display.

Alternative names None.
Size 80in.
Distribution Indo-China, Malaysia, Borneo, Sumatra, Thailand.
Habitat Lowland and hill forest.
Diet Fallen fruit, ants slugs, snails, meat, insects.

GOLDEN PHEASANT CHRYSOLOPHUS PICTUS

Dark green upper back, crown and crest golden yellow. Tips of tail coverts scarlet; ruff light orange barred black, underparts scarlet. Bill and facial skin yellow. Needs shelter as well as outside habitat. Keep in pairs or as a single specimen. Reluctant to fly.

Alternative names None.
Size 44in.
Distribution Central China, Great Britain.
Habitat Rocky hills, covered with bamboo or scrub.
Diet Seeds, leaves, shoots, insects.

SILVER PHEASANT LOPHURA NYCTHEMERA

These birds have a long white tail, red face, long black crest. The upper parts are white, lined with black. Yellow bill and red legs. They need shelter and an outside habitat. Polygamous, several hens can be kept with one cock bird. A poor game bird as they do not fly.

Alternative names None.
Size 50in.
Distribution Southern China, Burma, Indo-China, Hainan.
Habitat Grassland bordered by forest.
Diet Includes beetles, flower petals, grass, leaves and animal and vegetable matter.

LADY AMHERST'S PHEASANT CHRYSOLOPHUS AMHERSTIAE

Blue-green mantle and scapulars, yellow back and orange rump. Central tail feathers white barred in black, wings shiny blue, neck ruff white with dark blue margins. Needs shelter and an outside habitat. Most elusive of true pheasants, rarely emerging from thickets of habitat.

Alternative names None.
Size 68in.
Distribution Tibet, China, Burma. Introduced to Great Britain.
Habitat Bamboo thickets, in rocky mountains, woods and scrub.
Diet Bamboo shoots, small animals, aquatic animals.

REEVE'S PHEASANT SYRMATICUS REEVESI

Has a short body and a very long tail. Head and neck white, with black band from bill to nape. Body color yellow and marked with buff, brown, gray and black. Better to keep two hens with one cock bird and provide shelter in an outside habitat. Strong and hardy birds.

Alternative names None.
Size 84in.
Distribution China.
Habitat Suitable game bird to introduce into forested or hilly country.
Diet Insects and seeds.

RED-LEGGED PARTRIDGE SALECTORIS RUFA

Red legs and bill, the upper parts mouse-brown fading to buff belly, gray throat, white cheeks and over eye, throat bordered with black. They run rather than fly and call when they are about to fly. Often perch at height.

Alternative names None.
Size 13in.
Distribution France and Iberia; introduced to Great Britain, Azores, Madeira, Canaries.
Habitat Lowland scrub, sunny hillsides, vineyards, heaths.
Diet Stems, leaves, buds, berries, grass seeds, insects, spiders.

BARBARY DOVE STREPTOPELIA RISORIA

Light fawn with a black ring around the back of the neck. White offspring can occur, as well as apricot varieties and frilled forms. House indoors in winter. Tame and friendly to other small birds but can be aggressive to males of own species.

Alternative names Blond Ringdove, Ringdove, Domestic Ringdove, Domestic Collared Dove, Fawn Dove.
Size 9in.
Distribution Domesticated.
Habitat Suitable for an aviary.
Diet Mixtures for a domestic pigeon. Grit, cuttlefish, greenery.

DIAMOND DOVE GEOPELIA CUNEATA

Grayish-brown with white dots on wings, lighter gray on head and underside. Need a winter temperature of not less than 48°F. Separate birds to prevent continuous breeding. Lively, yet peaceful and easy to care for if kept in pairs.

Alternative names None.
Size 8 3/4in.
Distribution Australia.
Habitat Dry woodland and scrub.
Diet Feed on the ground with mixture of canary seeds, red and white millet, niger-thistle, sesame seed, wheat and poppy.

RED-VENTED BULBUL PYCNONOTUS CAFER

Black head and throat, blending to brown on neck, shoulders, breast and wings. Undertail coverts reddish, tail brown with white tips. Beak and legs blackish. House indoors in lightly heated area in winter. Tolerant of other species if kept singly. May sing if excited.

Alternative names None.
Size 8 1/2in.
Distribution India, Southeast Asia.
Habitat Farmland, near villages.
Diet Fruit, softbill food or mynah pellets, live food.

WHITE-EARED BULBUL PYCNONOTUS LEUCOTIS

White neck, breast sides and bell, darker grayish-brown on top, yellowish at vent. Often in large groups, intolerant of cold, they should be housed in a heated area in the winter. They are lively, inquisitive and tame.

Alternative names Yellow-Vented Bulbul.
Size 7in.
Distribution Iran to West Pakistan.
Habitat Wooded areas near water, near people in winter. Can damage fruit crops.
Diet Fruit, softbill food, mynah pellets, live food.

GOLDEN-FRONTED LEAFBIRD CHLOROPSIS AURIFRONS

Dark green body, underside and tail bright grass-green. Yellow crown, blue throat, steel-blue legs, black beak. Molts in autumn and dislikes cold, damp weather. Move inside before winter develops, Sing beautifully, enjoy bathing. Drinks a lot and makes a mess feeding. Quick tempered, and can be aggressive towards other birds.

Alternative names Fruitsucker.
Size 8in.
Distribution Himalayan region of India, Burma, Sumatra.
Habitat Forest, scrub.
Diet Fruit, nectar, insects, live food.

PEKIN ROBIN LEIOTHRIX LUTEA

Greenish-gray head and neck. Red flight feathers with black and yellow bands. Yellow throat blending to orange chest. Red beak. More than one pair in cage or aviary leads to fighting. Mealworms fed during nesting may cause birds to throw their eggs out and start breeding again. Beautiful singers.

Alternative names Red-Billed Leiothrix, Japanese Nightingale.
Size 6in.
Distribution Himalayas, Indo-China.
Habitat Heavily wooded areas.
Diet Mealworm, ant pupae, millet, hemp, boiled eggs, fruit, lettuce, spinach.

SILVER-EARED MESIA LEIOTHRIX ARGENTAURIS

Orange-yellow underparts, blending to red throat, rump and undertail. Yellow beak, red eyes, mantle olive with red. The male's full, deep call is too loud for indoors. Good breeder, tolerant of other birds in a community aviary.

Alternative names None.
Size 7in.
Distribution Nepal, Indo-China, Sumatra.
Habitat Mountain forests, except in winter when it descends to lower terrain.
Diet Mealworm, ant pupeae, millet, hemp, boiled eggs, fruit, lettuce, spinach.

INDIAN WHITE-EYED ZOSTEROPS ZOSTEROPS PALPEBROSA

Named after the white feathers around the eye. Olive on head and neck, blending to bright yellow underside. Food needs to be placed on a small table. Low tolerance of temperature changes. Keep indoors in winter. Bathing an absolute must.

Alternative names Oriental Zosterops, Indian White-Eye.
Size 6in.
Distribution India, Sri Lanka, Indo-China, Greater Sunda Islands.
Habitat Lowland woods.
Diet Insects, larvae, berries, fruit, cooked rice, sponge cake, carrots.

GREATER HILL MYNAH GRACULA RELIGIOSA

Black body with metallic sheen on back; orange beak, flights marked with white. Ear coverts covered by folds of yellow skin. Daily bathing in a dog sized bowl, keeps plumage clean. Lots of sunlight and well balanced diet needed to prevent convulsions. Change newspaper in cage at least daily and wash down perches. Has superior powers of mimicry.

Alternative names Hill Mynah Bird.
Size 18in.
Distribution India, Asia, Indonesia.
Habitat Woods, forests, near water.
Diet Fruit, mealworms, insects, dried fruits, softbill pellets.

SUPERB SPREO STARLING LAMPROTORNIS OR SPREO SUPERBUS

Metallic blue-green color, head black wings green with black spots and reddish underparts. White on undertail coverts, axilliaries and underwing. Breeds readily in aviary, so remove young of first brood when second is started. Has a chattering call, loud alarm.

Alternative names None.
Size 8in.
Distribution Somalia, Ethiopia, Sudan, East Africa.
Habitat Thornbush and acacia.
Diet Fruit, live foods.

SHAMA THRUSH COPSYCHUS MALABARICUS

Bluish-black body with white rump and sides of tail. Chestnut underparts, legs deep yellow. Separate pair from other birds if breeding. Attractive voice. Once acclimatized, can spend winter in a draft-free aviary if shelter is provided.

Alternative names Indian Nightingale.
Size 11in.
Distribution India, Indo-China, Sri Lanka, Burma, Thailand, China.
Habitat Nests in holes and cracks.
Diet Egg, hairless caterpillars, raw minced beef, thrush food, worms, insects.

PARADISE TANAGER TANGARA CHILENSIS

Black neck, shoulders, back and tail with brilliant sky blue on breast, belly and wing coverts. Yellowish-green head and red or yellow-red rump. Cover bottom of cage with absorbent paper to catch watery droppings caused by their sweet, juicy diet. Need a large, well-planted aviary or cage with washing facilities.

Alternative names None.
Size 5in.
Distribution South America, Bolivia, Brazil.
Habitat Forests and woodland.
Diet Fruit, insects.

SUPERB TANAGER TANGARA FASTUOSA

Overall black with purple-blue sheen on shoulders and tail. Has a 'ski-mask' hood of bluish-green with eye and beak black. Rump and underside orange. Keep newly imported birds at constant 77°F until acclimatized. Hose down daily and provide room-temperature bath water. Tame, tolerant birds for cage or aviary.

Alternative names Orange-Rumped Tanager.
Size 5 1/2in.
Distribution East Brazil.
Habitat Forests, high in trees.
Diet Fruit, rusk crumbs, ant pupae, red meat, boiled eggs, grated carrots.

CUVIER'S TOUCAN RAMPHASTOS CUVIERI

Black body with white around the eyes and down breast, bordered in red. Undertail red with yellow accent, black beak with yellow border. Diet must be low in fat as toucans are at risk from athereosclerosis. Does not behave well with other birds. Inquisitive and calm, loves to bathe often. Unable to mimic the human voice.

Alternative names None.
Size 18in.
Distribution South America.
Habitat Tropical rain forests.
Diet Fresh and dried fruit, insects, white bread, soaked rice.

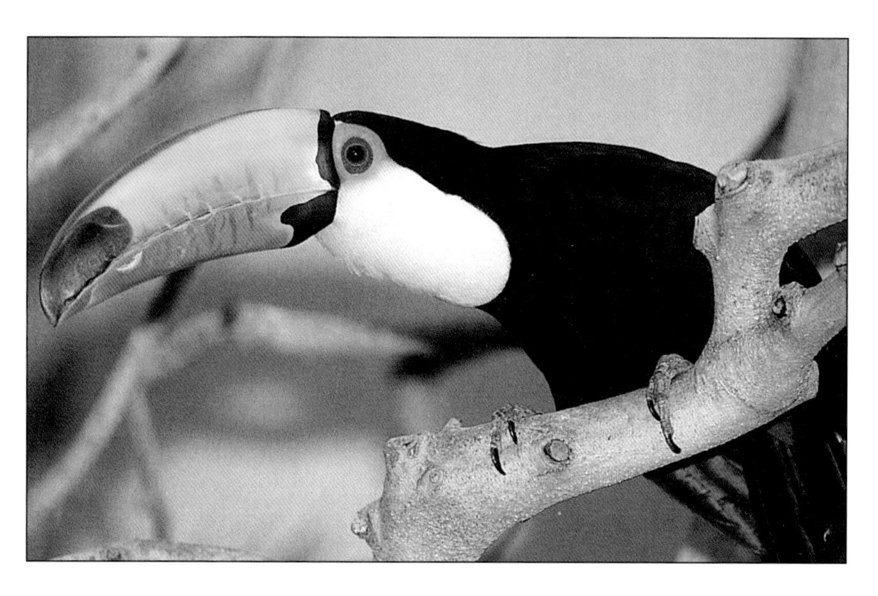

TOCO TOUCAN RAMPHISTIDAE TOCO

Distinguishing feature is a large beak, about a quarter of the total body length; it appears weighty, but is actually light as it has a honeycombed construction. Lacks 'beard' feathers around beak and feathers around eye. Has a long tongue frayed at the edges. Wings are short and, like tail, are rounded. Be sure that diet is low in fat since toucans tend to be at risk from athereosclerosis. Does not behave well with fellow species or small birds, particularly at feeding time.

Alternative names None.
Size 22in.
Distribution South America.
Habitat Tropical rain forests.
Diet Fresh and dried fruit, insects.

Index

Alphabetical listing of common names.